55 Of The Most Beautiful
Classical Piano

Solos

Masterpieces of Music

Contents

Solfeggio in D Major

Johann Christoph Friedrich Bach

March in D Major (BWV Anh. 122)

from the notebook for Anna Magdalena Bach

Johann Sebastian Bach

March in G Major (BWV Anh. 124)

from the notebook for Anna Magdalena Bach

Johann Sebastian Bach

63.

Invention No. 4 in D Minor (BWV 775)

from the notebook for Anna Magdalena Bach

Johann Sebastian Bach

Invention No. 8 in F Major (BWV 779)

Johann Sebastian Bach

Invention No. 13 in A Minor (BWV 784)

Johann Sebastian Bach

Minuet in G Major (BWV 116)

from the notebook for Anna Magdalena Bach

Johann Sebastian Bach

Polonaise in G Minor (BWV Anh. 119)

Johann Sebastian Bach

Praeabmulum 1 in C Major (BWV 924)

Johann Sebastian Bach

Prelude in C Minor (BWV 999)

Johann Sebastian Bach

With movement

Prelude in C Major (BWV 846)

Andante

Johann Sebastian Bach

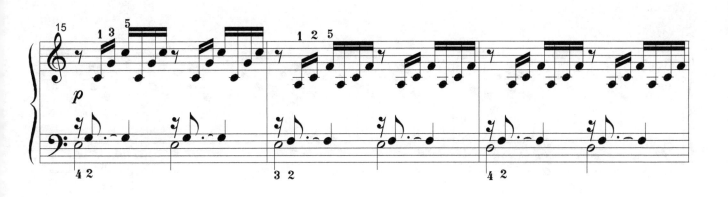

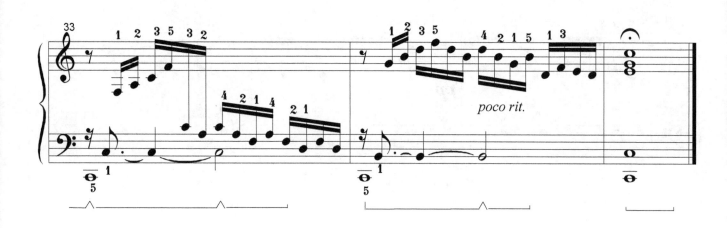

Musette in D Major (BWV Anh. 126)

from the notebook for Anna Magdalena Bach

Johann Sebastian Bach

For Elise A Minor (WoO. 59)

Bagatelle No. 25

Ludwig van Beethoven

Sonate in G Major (Op. 49, No. 20)

Ludwig van Beethoven

Sonatina in F Major (Anh. 5, No. 2)

Allegro assai

Ludwig van Beethoven

Rondo

Allegro

Sonatina in G Major (Anh. 5, No. 1)

Moderato

Arabesque (Op. 100, No. 2)

Johann Friedrich Burgmuller

Tarantelle (Op. 100, No. 20)

Johann Friedrich Burgmuller

Ballade (Op. 100, No. 15)

Allegro con brio

Johann Friedrich Burgmuller

Polonaise in G Minor (B1)

Allegro ma non troppo

Frederic Chopin

fine

d.c. al fine

52

Prelude in E Minor (Op. 28, No. 4)

Frederic Chopin

Prelude in D-flat Major (Op. 28, No. 15)

Frederic Chopin

Poco più animato

sotto voce

una corda

p *cresc.- - - -*

tre corde

ff

dim.- - -

Prelude in B Minor (Op. 28, No. 6)

Frederic Chopin

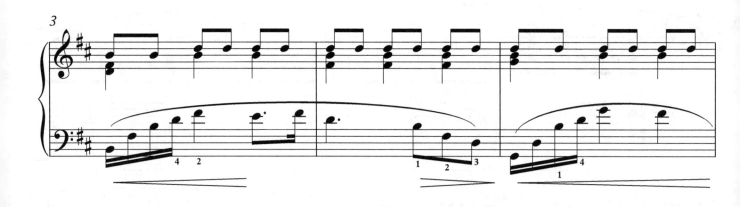

Sonatina 1 in C Major (Op. 36, No. 1)

Muzio Clementi

Andante

The Little Nigar (Op. 28, No. 6)

Claude Debussy

Arietta (Op. 12, No. 1)

Poco Andante e sostenuto

Edvard Grieg

Norwegian Melody (Op. 12, No. 6)

Edvard Grieg

Chaconne from Suite in D Minor (HWV 448, No. 23)

George Frideric Handel

Variation II

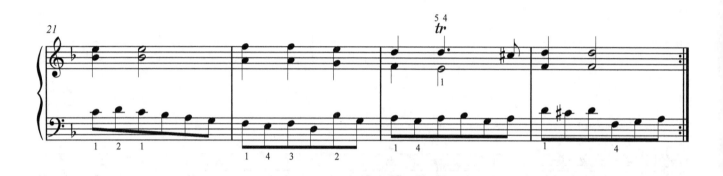

Variation III

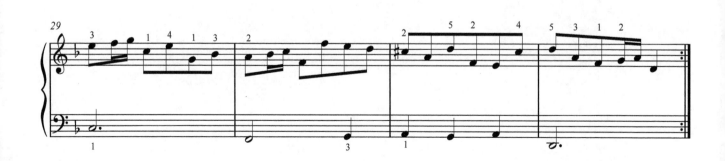

Variation IV

Variation V

Variation VI

Variation VII

Suite in D Minor (HWV 437)

George Frideric Handel

Allmande

Sarabande

Gigue

Minuet in F Major

Franz Joseph Haydn

Variations on an Austrian Folk Song (Op. 42, No. 1)

Friedrich Kuhlau

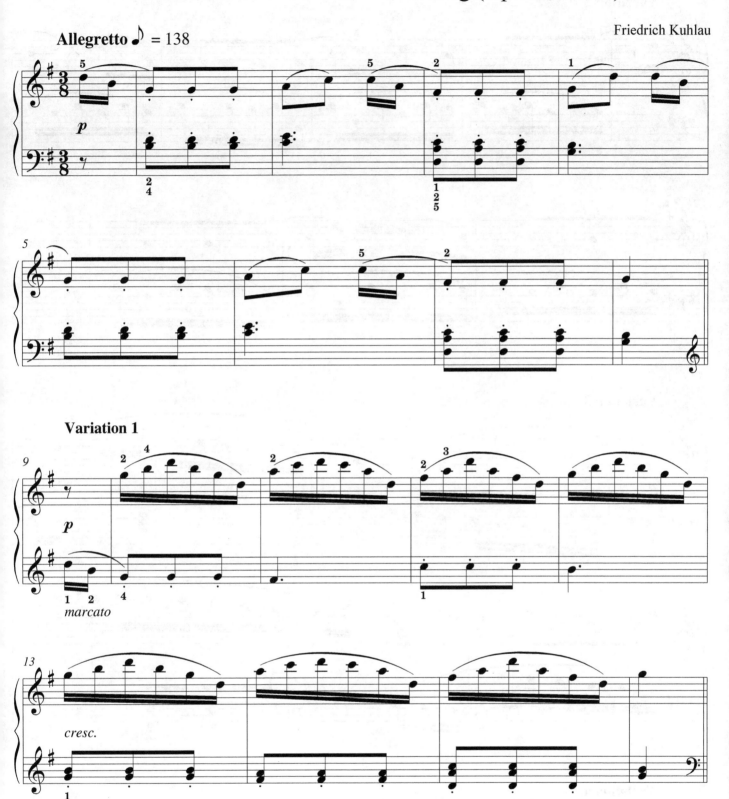

Variation 2

Variation 3

Variation 4

Variation 5

Variation 6

Song Without Words (Op. 30, No. 3)

Felix Mendelssohn Bartholdy

Song Without Words (Op. 19, No. 6)

Venetian Gondola Song

Felix Mendelssohn Bartholdy

Song Without Words (Op. 30, No. 6)

Venetian Gondola Song

Felix Mendelssohn Bartholdy

Allegro in B-Flat Major (K. 3)

for Pianoforte

Wolfgang Amadeus Mozart

Minuet in C Major (K. 6)

For Piano

Wolfgang Amadeus Mozart

Allegro

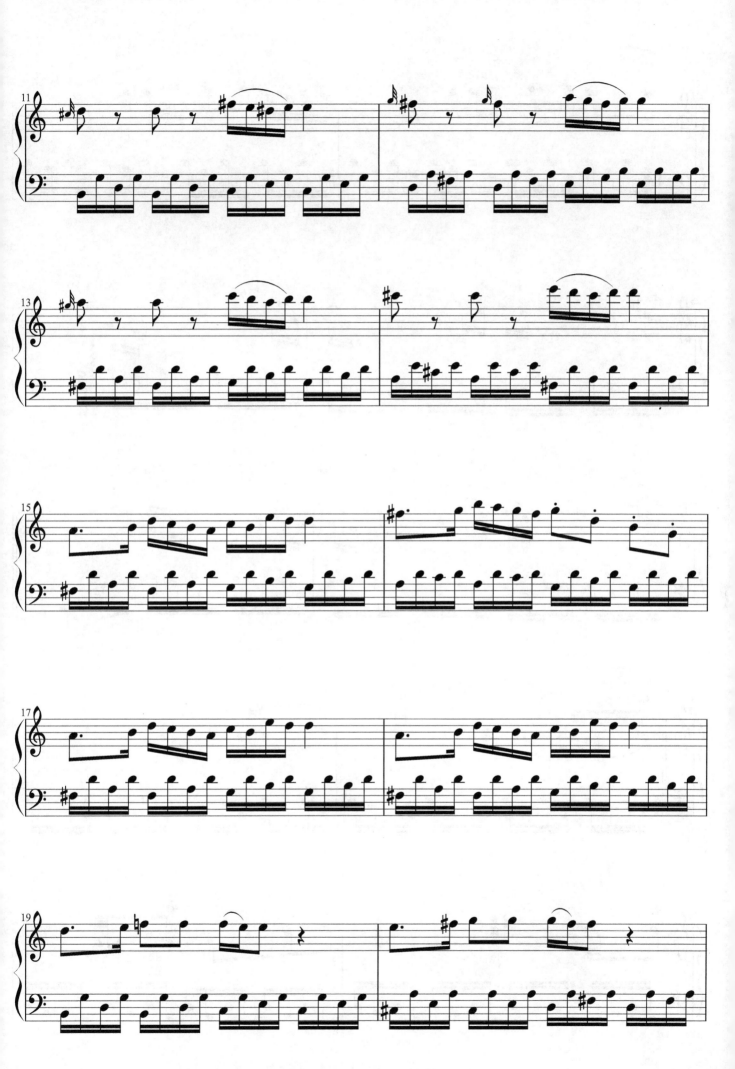

Andante

Minuet 1.)

Minuet 2.)

Allegretto

Minuet in F Major (K. 2)

Wolfgang Amadeus Mozart

Minuet in F Major (K. 5)

Wolfgang Amadeus Mozart

Minuet in G Major (K. 1)

for Piano

Wolfgang Amadeus Mozart

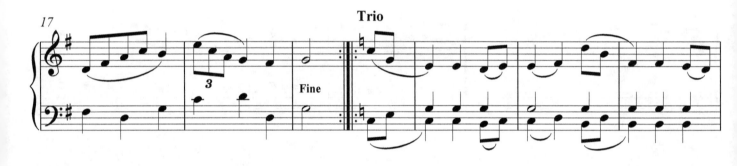

Trio

Fine

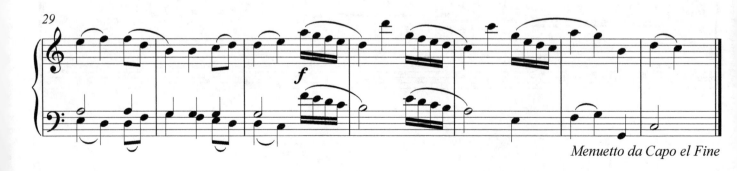

Menuetto da Capo el Fine

Piano Sonata No. 11 in A Major (K. 331/3)

"Alla Turca"

Wolfgang Amadeus Mozart

Sonate in C Major (K. 545)

Allegro

Wolfgang Amadeus Mozart

124

Fugue in A Minor (P 162)

Johann Pachelbel

Minuet in G Major (BWV Anh. 114)

Christian Petzold

Gymnopedie No. 1

Eric Satie

Scenes from Childhood (Op. 15, No. 4)

Robert Alexander Schumann

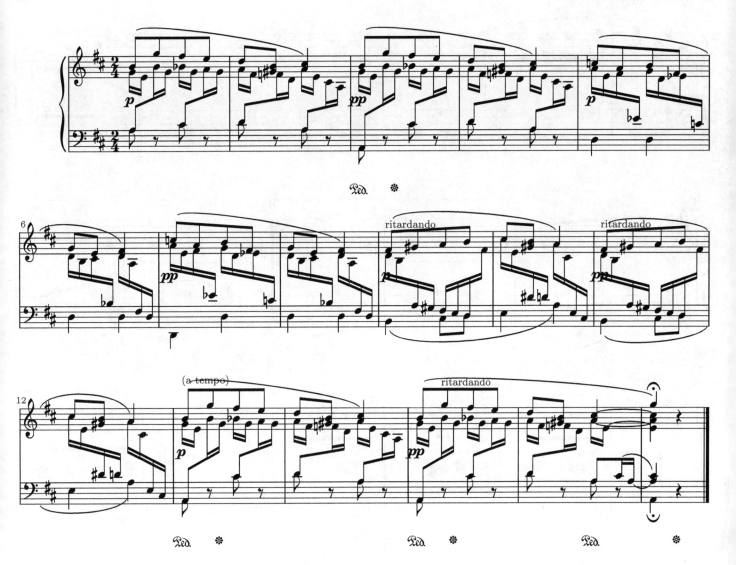

First Loss (Op. 68, No. 16)

Robert Alexander Schumann

Siciliana (Op. 68, No. 11)

Album for the Young

Robert Alexander Schumann

Espiègle

1.

(Comme au début et sans
répétitions jusqu'à la fin.)

(Fin.)

Scenes from Childhood (Op. 15, No. 7)

Träumerei

Robert Alexander Schumann

The Wild Horseman (Op. 68, No. 8)

Robert Alexander Schumann

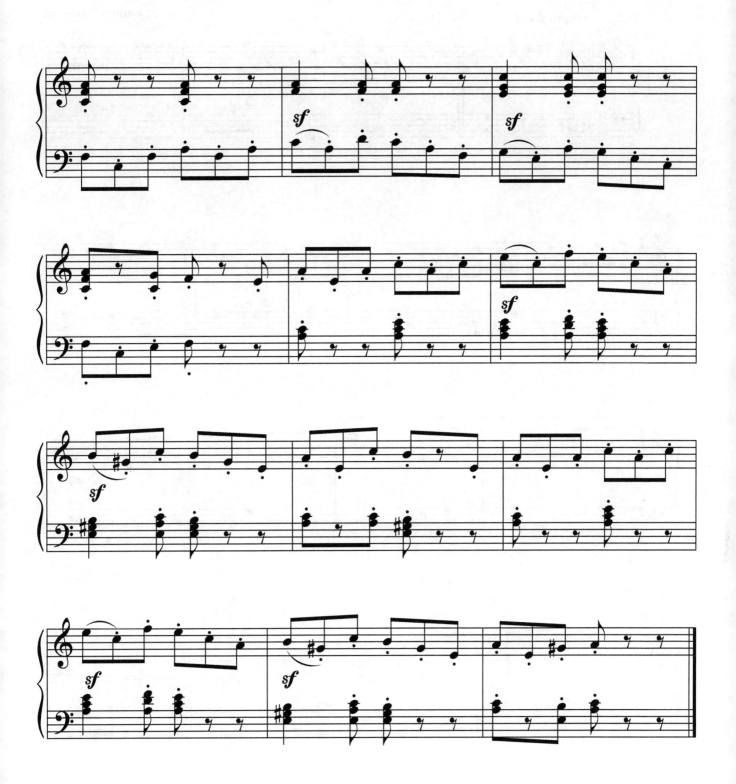

Gigue in G Major

Georg Philipp Telemann

The Sick Doll (Op. 39, No. 7)

Pyotr Ilyich Tchaikovsky

Old French Song (Op. 39, No. 16)

Pyotr Ilyich Tchaikovsky

Andantino

The Doll's Funeral (Op. 39, No. 7)

Pyotr Ilyich Tchaikovsky

The New Doll (Op. 39, No. 6)

Pyotr Ilyich Tchaikovsky

Italian Song (Op. 39, No. 15)

CPSIA information can be obtained
at www.ICGtesting.com
Printed in the USA
LVHW061055050520
655039LV00015B/2209